Hello Kitty®

FRIENDSHIP DOODLES

CREATE AND COMPLETE SUPERSWEET PICTURES

RP|KIDS
PHILADELPHIA · LONDON

Printed in China

9 8 7 6 5
Digit on the right indicates the number of this printing

Library of Congress Control Number: 2010925037

ISBN 978-0-7624-3971-3

Cover and interior design by Whitney Manger
Written and edited by Jordana Tusman
Typography: Chowderhead, Funnybone, and Univers

Published by Running Press Kids
an imprint of Running Press Book Publishers
2300 Chestnut Street
Philadelphia, PA 19103-4371

Visit us on the web!
www.runningpress.com
www.sanrio.com

Hello Kitty is at the park with her best friends.
Can you draw Tippy on the other end of the see-saw?

Hello Kitty and her friends are at school.
Can you draw her classmates sitting at their desks?

Hello Kitty and Tammy are resting on the grass
and imagining funny shapes in the clouds.
What kinds of shapes and objects do you see in the sky?

Hello Kitty and Mimmy are picking pretty flowers for Mama.
Can you draw flowers in their baskets?

Hello Kitty and Thomas are eating apple pie.
Can you draw a big pie on the table for them to eat?

Hello Kitty and Tracy are bike riding.
Who do they see on their ride?

Hello Kitty and her friends are playing soccer.
Can you draw the other players on the field?

PLAY
Don,t
Tin

Hello Kitty is on a train with her friends.
Can you draw other passengers?

Hello Kitty and Mimmy are taking a dance class together.
Can you draw Mimmy dancing?

Hello Kitty and Thomas are drinking lemonade on a sunny day.
Draw them drinking big glasses of lemonade.

Hello Kitty and her friends are on their way to school.
Who is on the bus and who is waiting at the bus stop?

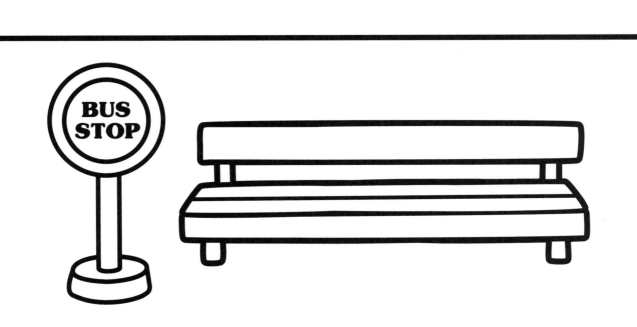

Hello Kitty and Rorry are making art projects together.
What masterpieces have they created?

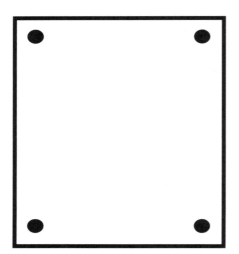

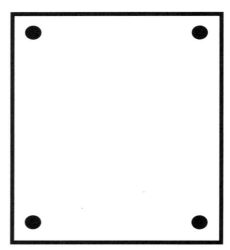

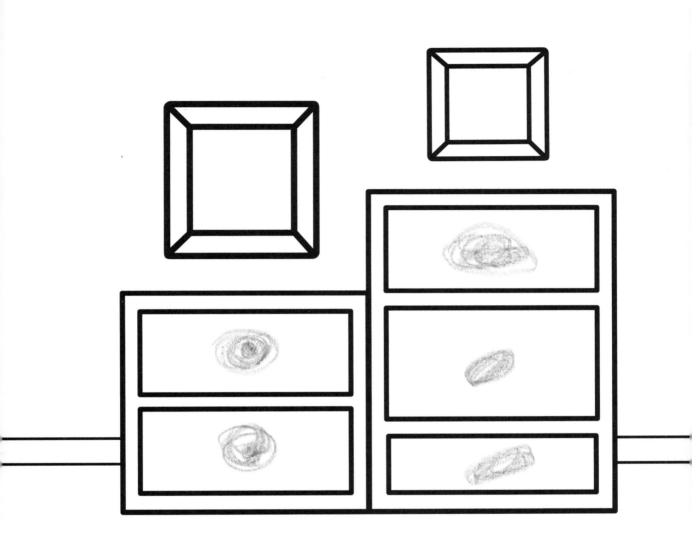

Hello Kitty and Joey are looking at the stars
through their telescope.
How many stars do you see in the sky?

Hello Kitty and Mimmy are cooking together.
What have they made for dinner tonight?

Hello Kitty and Dear Daniel are driving in a car.
Where are they going?

Hello Kitty and Joey are writing their names in fun letters.
Can you write their names in fun letters?

Hello Kitty and Mimmy are practicing their lines for the school play.
Can you draw them in costume?

Hello Kitty and her friends are feeding the animals at the farm.
What animals are they feeding?

Papa is painting with Hello Kitty and Mimmy.
What are they painting today?

Hello Kitty and her friends are playing in the sand.
Can you draw the castles they've made?

Hello Kitty and Mimmy are spending time in the park.
Can you draw them sitting on the bench?

Hello Kitty and Jodie are wearing fun hats.
Can you draw Jody's hat?

Hello Kitty and her friends are playing with the neighborhood dogs.
Can you draw them?

Hello Kitty and Thomas are taking turns pushing
each other on the tire swing.

Can you draw Hello Kitty pushing Thomas?

Hello Kitty is at a diner with her friend.
Can you draw the milkshake they are sharing?

Hello Kitty and Fifi are looking at a rainbow.
Can you color in the rainbow and draw a pot of gold at the end?

Hello Kitty and Mimmy are trying on different outfits.
Can you draw the clothes on the hangers?

Hello Kitty and Fifi are playing with their teddy bears.
Can you draw a picture of your favorite stuffed animal?

Hello Kitty and Mimmy get big lollipops at the doctor's office after their checkups.
Can you draw big lollipops for them?

Hello Kitty and Joey are doodling on the chalkboards.
What do their doodles look like?

Hello Kitty and Dear Daniel are at a country fair.
Can you draw the ferris wheel?

What else do you see?

This is Hello Kitty's house.
Can you draw her friends waving from the windows?

Hello Kitty and Joey are drawing pictures together.
What drawings have they made today?

Hello Kitty and Mimmy are scared by a thunderstorm.
Grandma brings them treats so they won't be afraid.
What snacks are on Grandma's tray?

Hello Kitty and Tippy are feeding the ducks by the pond.

How many ducks do you see?

Hello Kitty and her friends are having a campfire.

Can you draw Hello Kitty's friends sitting with her around the fire?

Hello Kitty and her friends are going to the beach.
Who do you see playing on the sand and splashing in the water?

Hello Kitty and Tippy are making snow angels together.
Can you draw the angels they made in the snow?

Hello Kitty and her friends are at a picnic.
What foods are they eating?